MICROBES
and
BACTERIA

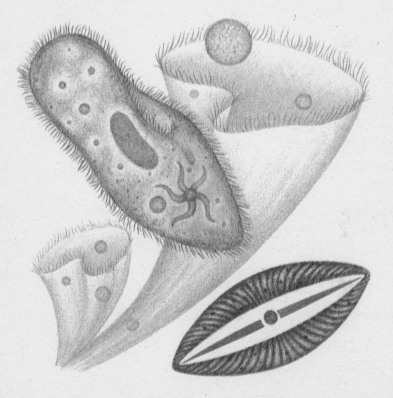

Troll Associates

MICROBES
and
BACTERIA

by Francene Sabin

Illustrated by Alexis Batista

Troll Associates

Library of Congress Cataloging in Publication Data

Sabin, Francene.
    Microbes and bacteria.

    Summary: A brief introduction to the invisible world of
microbes and bacteria, what scientists have found out
about these tiny creatures, and their importance to our
daily life.
    1. Micro-organisms—Juvenile literature. [1. Micro-
organisms. 2. Microbiology] I. Batista, Alexis, ill.
II. Title.
QR57.S23   1984   576   84-2749
ISBN 0-8167-0232-2 (lib. bdg.)
ISBN 0-8167-0233-0 (pbk.)

All around us are living things we cannot see. In the earth, in the air, in the water, billions and billions of these tiny microbes exist. Microbes are life forms too small to be seen by the human eye. In fact, some of them are so small that we cannot see them even through the most powerful microscope.

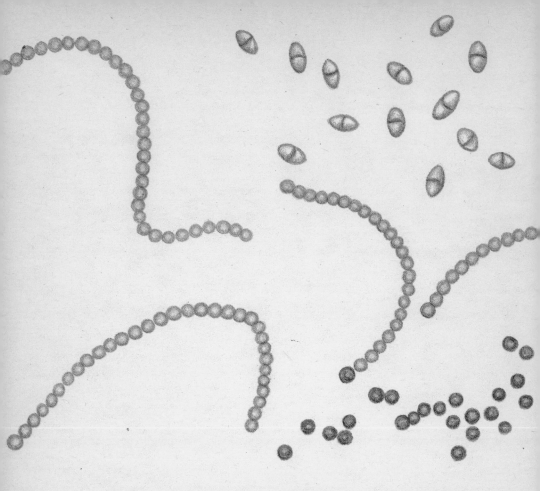

There are hundreds of thousands of different microbe species. Under a microscope, some look like clear, liquid-filled bags that are constantly changing shape. Some look like strings of beads. Some look like worms, bunches of grapes, or flowers with stems. Others look like pom-poms or thin twigs. And still others look like brightly colored jewels or glittering crystals.

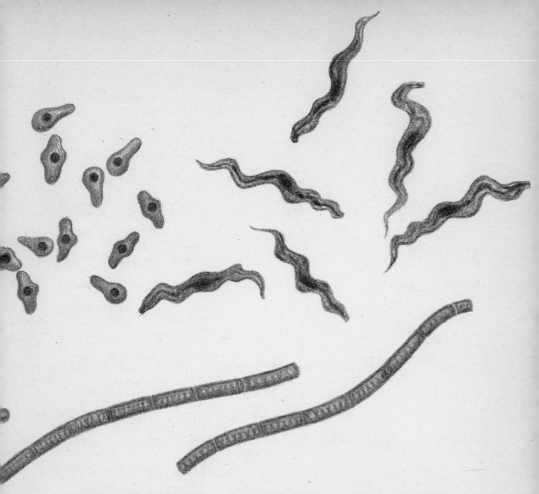

Microbiologists, scientists who study microbes, divide these tiny life forms into different groups. One group is made up of *protozoans*, which means "first animals." Protozoans are simple, one-celled forms of animal life. Another group is the *algae*, which are simple, one-celled forms of plant life. There are also *fungi, slime molds, bacteria, rickettsiae,* and *viruses.*

Microbes were probably the first life forms on Earth. But they weren't discovered until about three hundred years ago. It was then that a Dutchman named Anton van Leeuwenhoek, using a microscope he had made himself, saw the tiny moving creatures. He called them *animalcules*, which means "little beasties." But van Leeuwenhoek's microscope was a crude instrument, and with it he could see only the largest microbes.

As the years went by, other people constructed more powerful microscopes, which made many more kinds of microbes visible. At the same time, scientists were learning how to grow microbes in laboratories. This was how the modern science of microbiology was developed.

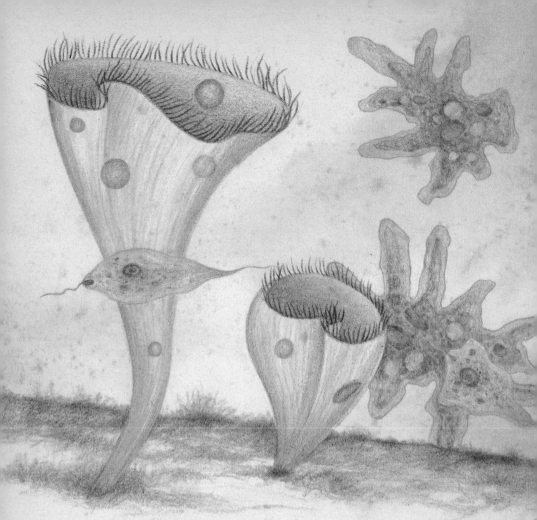

Today, microbiologists study the microbes that cause disease and those that cure disease. They study the microbes that help plants grow in the soil and the microbes that live in the seas. They study microbes that make our food and microbes that decay food.

Using a simple, single-lens microscope, van Leeuwenhoek was able to study only the largest microbes, such as protozoans, algae, and some bacteria. The first microbes he saw were protozoans, which he found in rainwater collected in a barrel.

Among these protozoans was one called paramecium. A paramecium is a commonly found, one-celled animal shaped like a shoe. It is covered with fine hairs called cilia. The paramecium uses its cilia like oars to move through its watery world. These microscopic animals feed on bacteria and other protozoans.

Another common protozoan is the amoeba. An amoeba takes different shapes as it moves through its wet environment. When an amoeba senses it is near food, such as a bacterium, it goes in that direction. To do this, the amoeba stretches out a *pseudopod*, or "false foot." The amoeba continues to move by pseudopod action until it is right next to the food. Then the pseudopods stretch out and around the food, trapping it. And the amoeba eats the bacterium.

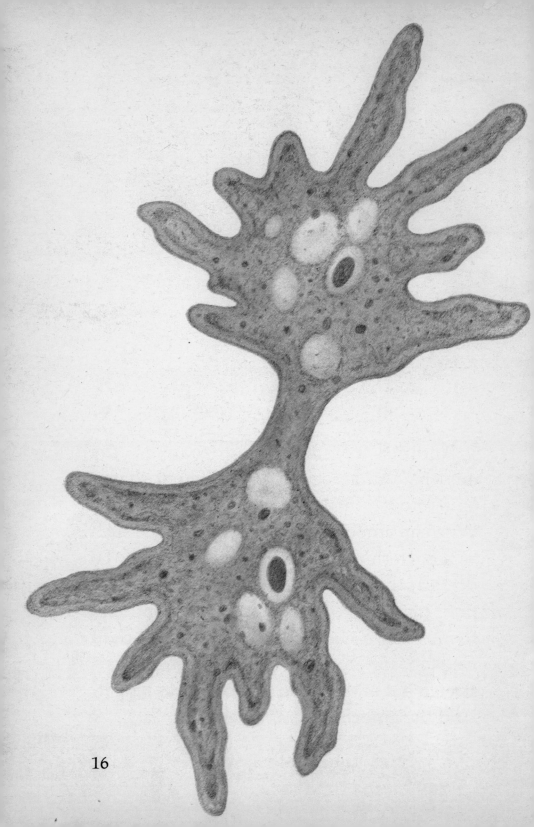

16

Protozoans like the paramecium and the amoeba reproduce by cell division. When the cell divides, the nucleus of the cell divides in half. The nucleus of a protozoan, like the nucleus of any other living cell, holds the chemical information that the cell needs to function. Without a nucleus a cell cannot digest food, grow, or reproduce itself.

When a protozoan divides, two smaller cells are created. Each has a complete nucleus and surrounding body. In fact, they are exactly the same as each other and the cell that gave rise to them. If these two survive, they will grow and also divide themselves, making four protozoans that are exactly the same.

Protozoans and other microbes reproduce themselves at an extremely fast rate. There can be thousands of generations of a particular microbe in just one day. But most of the cells do not live very long. Some cannot find food; some become food for other creatures; and some dry up.

Most algae also reproduce themselves by splitting in two. But unlike protozoans, algae are plants. And like the larger plants we see every day, such as trees, algae make their food. They do this through a process called photosynthesis. In photosynthesis, a plant uses sunlight to change water and carbon-dioxide gas into food.

Algae come in many different forms. Some are single-celled green balls. Some grow in long, thin chains of cells. Some grow together in clumps or clusters. Some, known as diatoms, even have shells! But all algae are plants that need water to survive.

Fungi and slime molds are microbes that reproduce by sending out spores. A spore is a cell that is a bit like a plant seed. When a spore lands in a moist place, it sends out little threads. The fungus or slime mold feeds through these threads. They feed on dead plant and animal matter and on bacteria. In nature, the fungi and slime molds help us by breaking down this dead matter into chemicals. These chemicals are used by new, growing plants.

The medical uses of molds are very important to human beings, too. Penicillin and many other antibiotics are molds that feed on bacteria. Penicillin was discovered when Alexander Fleming, a Scottish scientist, found a spot of mold growing in a dish of disease-causing bacteria. Dr. Fleming noticed that where the mold was spreading, the bacteria were disappearing. In time, this discovery led to the development of a wide range of disease-fighting antibiotics.

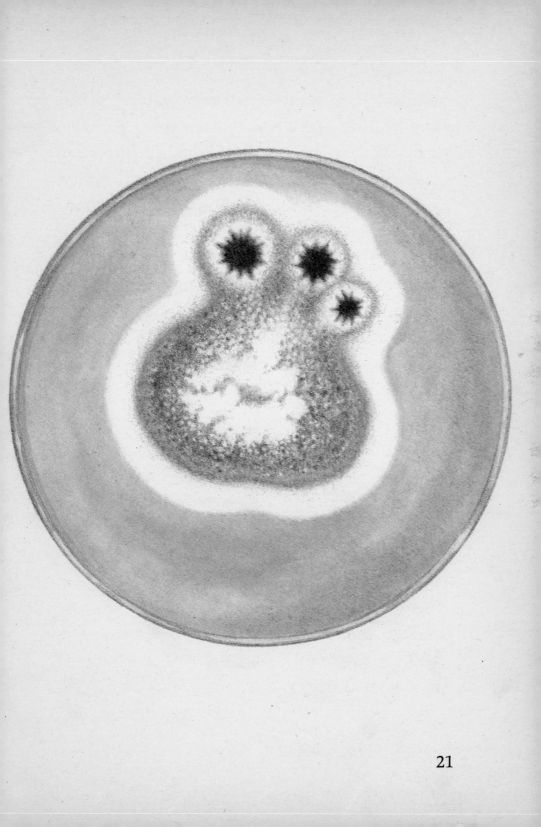

Antibiotics removed the threat of some diseases that once were incurable. Among these diseases are tuberculosis, different kinds of pneumonia, diphtheria, and many common infections, such as strep throat. Each of these is caused by a different type of bacterium.

Bacteria are neither plants nor animals. A bacterium does have a nucleus, but it is not enclosed in a thin tissue, the way a nucleus of a plant or animal cell is.

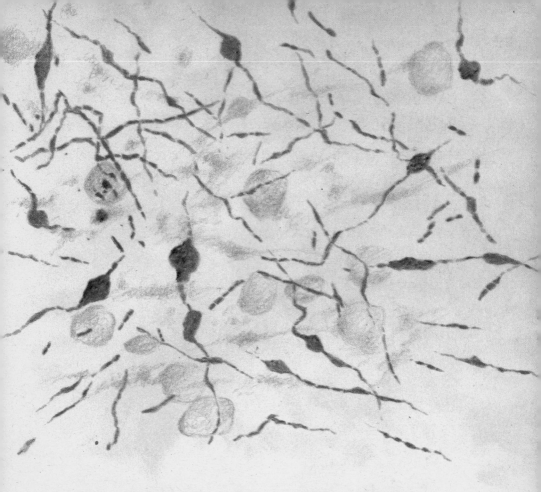

Some bacteria feed on other organisms, the way animals do. Some bacteria make their own food, the way plants do. And some bacteria do both. There are bacteria that need air in order to survive, and others that exist without air. Some bacteria move by themselves, and some cannot move. Bacteria vary greatly in shape, color, size, and ways of existence.

Not all bacteria are harmful. In fact, most of them are helpful to us. Bacteria break down dead plant and animal matter for reuse in nature. Bacteria help nitrogen, an important chemical element, to form in soil. Plants cannot grow without nitrogen.

Bacteria are needed to make cheese out of milk and to make leather out of animal hides. Cows, sheep, and a number of other animals digest the grass they eat with the help of bacteria that live in their stomachs.

Bacteria are all around us. They are in the air we breathe, in the water we drink, in the food we eat, and on everything we touch. Since very few of these bacteria are dangerous to us, our bodies are seldom bothered by them.

Most of the time, when harmful bacteria do enter a human body, the body fights back and kills the invading microbes. To do this, the body uses white blood cells that surround and destroy the attacking bacteria.

Of course, we can help prevent harmful bacteria from entering our bodies by washing with soap, brushing our teeth regularly, avoiding eating spoiled food, and by treating bacterial infections promptly.

There are two kinds of microbes that are even smaller than bacteria. They are called rickettsiae and viruses. Both rickettsiae and viruses are parasites. This means that they live inside and feed on other kinds of cells. Typhus, a dread disease, is caused by rickettsiae that live in insects known as body lice. The smallest known microbes are called viruses. Viruses cause the common cold, smallpox, measles, and poliomyelitis.

There aren't any specific cures yet for viral diseases, but there are ways of dealing with them. Of course, ordinary colds do not need special attention—the body defends us against their viruses. Smallpox, measles, and polio, however, are more serious, so we try to prevent them.

We fight serious viral diseases by using vaccines. A vaccine is a tiny dose of the virus that causes the disease. When it is given, the vaccine helps a person's body build protective substances. These substances will fight off any invasion by the disease-causing virus.

The science of microbiology has come a long way since Anton van Leeuwenhoek first looked into his microscope. Yet many questions remain unanswered. The world of microbes is still filled with countless mysteries waiting to be solved.